How to Have More Time

Practical Ways to Put an End to
Constant Busyness and
Design a Time-Rich Lifestyle

By Martin Meadows

Download Another Book for Free

I want to thank you for buying my book and offer you another book (just as valuable as this one): *Grit: How to Keep Going When You Want to Give Up*, completely free.

Visit the link below to receive it:

http://www.profoundselfimprovement.com/havemoretime

In *Grit*, I'll tell you exactly how to stick to your goals, using proven methods from peak performers and science.

In addition to getting *Grit*, you'll also have an opportunity to get my new books for free, enter giveaways, and receive other valuable emails from me.

Again, here's the link to sign up:

http://www.profoundselfimprovement.com/havemoretime

Table of Contents

Prologue

"I don't have time."

When was the last time you heard that or said it yourself? A few days ago? Yesterday? Today?

Everyone is busy. Everybody wants more hours in the day.

Nobody can afford to simply *live* because there are still so many things to do and *oh I can't stop it's all so important.*

Chronic busyness creeps up on us like an epidemic disease. We work, work, work, and then it's too late to realize that, as John Lennon sang in "Beautiful Boy," "Life is what happens to you while you're busy making other plans."

If there's one common complaint I hear on a regular basis, it's "I don't have time." It makes me want to grab someone by the collar and yell in his face, "get yourself together!"

What do you think is the most precious currency we have in this world?

US Dollars?

Try again.

Gold?

Nope, sorry.

Perhaps real estate?

Wrong answer.

Time is the most precious currency we have in this world because it's the only finite resource that you can't buy. Everything else can be bought with money. If your time is up, your time is up – the Grim Reaper doesn't accept credit cards, checks, cash, gold, or real estate, no matter how rich you are.

Yet, so many people live their lives as though they'll live forever. They're so busy chasing money, they lose the only currency they have – their time and the freedom to spend it on the things that really matter.

I don't claim that money doesn't matter, though. Unemployed people have all the time in the world, but they don't have true time freedom, unless they're a part of a forgotten tribe in Papua New Guinea where the concept of money isn't as applicable as in the rest of the world.

Once you're past a certain level of income, though, chasing more money at the expense of losing what's most important – your time – is a ridiculous decision that perhaps leads to more money, but at the cost of overall happiness in life.

Numerous studies[1, 2, 3, 4] have shown that happiness isn't the function of things, but of experiences – and most notably time spent with family and friends.

A major finding of one of the longest studies on the quality of life, the Harvard Study of Adult Development[5], is that good relationships affect our happiness the most.

If you're constantly busy, how do you expect to have close relationships? A constant lack of time is a recipe for unhappiness in life – and that's just one of many reasons why busyness isn't the answer.

6

I refused to subscribe to the mindset of busyness. Instead, I structured my life in such a way that now I can do what I want, whenever I want (and no, the answer isn't constant idleness, but it isn't constant busyness, either).

I wrote this book because I hate hearing people saying "I don't have time." I'll give you practical solutions that worked for me that might also work for you – or help you come up with your own ideas that will help you get more hours in the day to do what you want, and not just *do more*.

In the following pages you'll learn what you can do to regain control over your time. We'll:

- explore the biggest time suck in your life and cover some practical ways to deal with it (trends show more and more people are starting to get it – you're about to find out the why and how),

- how to live a distraction-free life, or at least not let the distractions take over your entire day,

- how a materialistic lifestyle robs you of precious time and why it's a sure-fire way to attract unhappiness in your life,

- learn why exhaustion doesn't equal effectiveness (and even though it sounds obvious, you most likely also act in a counterintuitive way),

- how to structure your lifestyle for maximum time freedom – including both big and small life decisions that make all the difference,

- discover numerous unconventional ideas to create more time (and no, I will not share with you time management techniques that will only make you even more busy).

Would you like to finally stop saying you don't have time and be able to do what you want and when you want? If so, turn the page and let's discover the vast number of options to regain control over your day and reprioritize your life to have more time and happiness instead of more stuff and busyness.

Chapter 1: Your Biggest Time Suck

According to Gallup's annual Work and Education Survey, the average workweek for an adult American working full-time is 47 hours[6].

This number doesn't include commute time, which, according to another survey by Gallup, takes an average of 46 minutes per day[7]. In total, the average time spent at work and work-related tasks is closer to over 50 hours a week or 10 hours per workday.

Subtract 8 hours for sleep and you're left with 4 hours a day. Subtract another 1-2 hours for eating (including cooking time, shopping, or waiting in a restaurant), hygiene, daily chores, some exercise, and you're left with a generous one hour a day for everything else like actually living your life.

It's not an overstatement to say that a typical 9 to 5 job is the biggest time suck in your life. Even if you don't work in a typical 9 to 5 job and own your business or work as a freelancer, chances are you're still just as busy, if not more.

Of course, I don't mean to be ungrateful – in uncertain economic times, a stable job or a prospering business – even if it takes up the majority of your time – is a treasure.

However, it doesn't mean you should accept the situation as it is. You can still reduce your workload – while not neglecting your responsibilities, and in many cases tremendously improve your output.

In the following chapter, you'll find three subchapters – a subchapter for people working a 9 to 5 job with fixed hours, a subchapter for freelancers or people wanting to become one, and a final subchapter for entrepreneurs and people planning to launch their own businesses.

While I invite you to read all of the subchapters for various perspectives, if you're hard-pressed for time, read the section that applies to you the most.

Scenario #1: Your 9 to 5 Job Keeps You in Shackles

Let's set things clear: if you have a 9 to 5 job with fixed hours, time will most likely always be a scarce resource for you. You can optimize it slightly, though. There are two routes you can take depending on what you're willing to do:

1. You don't imagine your life without a 9 to 5 job

If you're unable to reduce the time spent at work, you can work on optimizing the energy you invest in the job so you can leave it less exhausted, and thus have more energy to get the most out of the time after work.

A Latvian company, Draugiem Group, conducted an analysis in which they used a time-tracking productivity app to see what sets apart their most productive employees when it comes to their habits at work[8].

It turned out that the more productive employees didn't work longer hours, as some would assume. Instead, they took regular breaks –averaging 17-minutes every 52 minutes. The most productive employees stepped away from their desks and spent their breaks away from email, social media, or shuffling papers. Instead, they chatted with their colleagues about non-work-related issues, took a walk, or read a book.

As a result, they not only had better results, but were also less exhausted after the entire day of work. Alternating between periods of 100% focus on work and 100% focus on rest helps you avoid distracting yourself in the middle of the job.

Consequently, you benefit from working with purpose while your body and brain benefit from not being forced to be "on" the entire time.

Consider introducing a similar schedule in your day job. As Dr. James A. Levine, professor of medicine at the Mayo Clinic says, "the work should break up the break"[9].

And if your boss is unhappy about it, send him a link to the article about the Latvian company or numerous other articles suggesting that the brain works better in short spurts.

We'll cover specific ways to deal with distractions in a later chapter dedicated to the subject. For now, think of ways you can split your work schedule in such a way that your brain and body get a break at least once an hour for a minimum of 5-10 minutes each.

Another technique to optimize your daily schedule is to try negotiating working from home.

If it takes you 30-60 minutes a day to get to and from work (and an additional 30-60 minutes to get yourself ready), and you could negotiate working from home even one or two days a week, that's an additional one or two hours you can spend doing something else.

A popular book, *4-Hour Workweek*, by Tim Ferriss provides a sample script and strategy you can follow to negotiate more flexible hours with your boss.

A 2015 Gallup survey shows that 37% of U.S. workers have telecommuted[10]. Considering the fact that this number amounted to just 9% in 1995, the trend of telecommuting is clear. We can only expect more and more people working from home – and more and more bosses willing to give it a go as long as productivity doesn't go down.

However, please keep in mind that working from home comes with its own challenges like the distractions you can experience while not being in a monitored office environment. We'll discuss them later.

In some companies there's also an option of working 10-hour workdays 4 days a week. It might be yet another way to optimize your schedule and have one extra day at home to take care of other chores, spend time with your family, or relax.

If you've ever entertained the thought of trying a different type of employment than a traditional 9 to 5 job with fixed hours, I strongly suggest pondering it.

2. You could consider other types of employment

If you're not dead-set on working a traditional 9 to 5 job with fixed hours, your options to have more time are richer.

Gaining freedom over your daily schedule – even if it's just a modicum of freedom by being able to shift your work hours by an hour or two to fix your schedule better – can result in substantial gains of additional free time.

Many jobs today – particularly in sales – don't require employees to work fixed hours or go to the office. What's more important than the hours you put in are the results you generate. As an additional bonus, these jobs can be more profitable and open up more career opportunities than your typical paper shuffling job.

Two other options are freelancing and entrepreneurship, covered in later sections.

For now, let's focus on more flexible jobs. According to a Forbes article on the 10 high-paying flexible jobs, the best options for people who are looking for a job allowing schedule flexibility are[11]:

1. Senior project management, IT, for workers with at least a bachelor's degree and 5 to 8 years of experience: $99,700 with 26% of workers telecommuting

2. Actuary: $94,600 with 93% of workers having a flexible schedule

3. Attorney/lawyer: $92,400 with 91% having a flexible schedule

4. Management consultant: $89,500 with 16% of workers telecommuting

5. Tax manager: $89,300 with 14% telecommuting

6. Security engineer, information systems: $87,000 with 23% telecommuting

7. Technical sales engineer: $85,200 with 20% telecommuting

8. Clinical Research Associate: $81,400 with 17% telecommuting and 85% having a flexible schedule

9. Regional sales manager: $80,300 with 17% telecommuting

10. Aerospace engineer: $79,600 with 84% having a flexible schedule

These are just some of the most lucrative flexible career choices that will allow you to make a lot of money while offering the possibility to have at least some control over your schedule.

As for general trends, a FlexJobs.com article on the most flexible careers for 2016 suggests the following areas[12]:

1. Medical care

2. Sales

3. Customer service

4. Administrative

5. Computer & IT

6. Education & Training

7. Accounting & Finance

8. Account Management

9. Data Entry

10. Bilingual jobs

If you're sure you don't want to continue on your current career path, consider entering one of the industries above to optimize your finances as well as finally have time to enjoy the perks of having money – and not just working more and more hours in an endless vicious cycle.

If you've ever considered quitting your job and going on your own, the following two subchapters are for you.

Scenario #2: A Freelancing Career
Is the First Step Towards Freedom

Another possible route to explore is starting a freelancing career and offering your services to other people or companies. While freelancers aren't necessarily "pure" entrepreneurs who can make money while they sleep, they usually have much more flexibility and freedom than people who have a boss.

More and more people are leaving their day jobs and becoming freelancers or contractors to their previous bosses. According to research conducted by Intuit, an American software company, by 2020, more than 40% of the American workforce will be independent workers: freelancers, contractors, and temporary employees[13].

The *Freelancing in America 2015 Report* shows that nearly 54 million Americans are now doing freelance work (half-time or full-time)[14].

Of the 7,107 freelancers who took part in the study, half said they wouldn't stop freelancing for any amount of money.

Moreover, 60% of freelancers who left their day jobs now earn more – and of those, 78% indicated they earned more freelancing within a year or less, thus dispelling any myths that it takes a lot of time to establish yourself as a freelancer.

Additionally, more than 33% of freelancers report that demand for their services increased in the past year, and nearly 50% expect their freelancing income to increase in the coming year.

Convinced yet?

The Internet, laptops, tablets, and smartphones have all made it easy to work from home, a café, or virtually anywhere you want.

The first obvious gain when you decide to launch a freelancing career is that you no longer have to commute if you perform a job that can be done remotely. In many cases, that's at least 5 to 10 hours a week more to spend as you wish.

You can even consider moving to a cheaper neighborhood farther away from the city center since you'll no longer need to commute every single day – and that can result in additional considerable financial savings as well, thus letting you work fewer hours while maintaining the same quality of life.

The second gain of becoming a freelancer is that you can control your own hours. Even if you keep working the same number of hours as at your previous job, you can set your own schedule so that you have more time when you need it.

For instance, you can "go" to work at 6 in the morning and be done by 2 in the afternoon. Or if you're a night owl, you can sleep until 9 AM and get your work done in the afternoon or in the late evening. It allows setting a more natural schedule that fits your preferences and daily habits better.

The third benefit of becoming an independent worker is that you can delegate parts of your job to other people, and ultimately –

transition from being a worker to being a full-fledged entrepreneur. In many cases, starting with a freelancing career, and then expanding it into a business is the best way to safely and cheaply launch a successful company.

If you're unsure whether you can become a full-time freelancer, take things slowly and start part-time – do a few jobs here and there on the weekends or in the evenings.

The easiest way to start is to create a professional profile on a freelancing platform like Upwork where you can find hundreds of new jobs posted each day.

"But I want more time – and you're telling me to start another job?" you might ask. Well – getting more time often resembles financial investments. You have to give something first to get a return. If I told you that after spending the next three months building your freelancing career you'd have a regular stream of flexible, less time-consuming jobs that would replace your day job income or double it, wouldn't such a sacrifice make sense?

"But I need my health insurance," you might say next, particularly if you're from the US. Well, all you need to do is ask 96 million of self-employed people in the US[15] how they handled this problem and do the same. Perhaps it is indeed a bit harder to have sufficient health insurance as a self-employed person. However, if so many people figured it out, couldn't you?

"But the income isn't stable," might be also on your mind. But is your day job income really that stable? Of course, you get your

17

check every week, every other week, or every month, and the amount is most likely always the same, while freelancing income varies.

However, if you work for somebody else, you never truly know what's going on behind the scenes. If you're self-employed, at least you're the one at the steering wheel and can still act when you notice you're rapidly approaching a cliff. Good luck rescuing the company you work for if it goes bankrupt.

Your excuse is of some merit, though. Freelancing income can indeed be much less stable as clients and jobs come and go. However, it all depends on your marketing skills and the quality of your work. Rest assured that the best freelancers in their fields never go hungry.

If You're Already a Freelancer and Can't Find Time

What if your freelancing reality isn't as beautiful as it's often painted, and you're still extremely busy and strapped for time?

It's usually a result of the three most common scenarios listed below. Please keep in mind that specific advice is beyond the scope of this book. The goal of this subsection is to merely give you some ideas how to regain control over your time as a freelancer.

1. You work like crazy just to have a steady stream of jobs.

A small survey of 643 freelancers conducted by Contently.net's magazine, The Freelancer, showed that the biggest obstacle by far – shared by 34.1% respondents – was securing more work[16].

Fortunately, this problem is relatively easy to solve – all it takes is either some time (for beginning freelancers who need to build their reputation) or learning a few marketing skills to guarantee a steady stream of jobs (for more experienced freelancers).

If you've just started out, consider taking some jobs for a very low fee or for free just to get a few positive reviews (if you get jobs through a freelancing platform) or to have a few good testimonials to put on your site. Most clients will never hire a freelancer who can't document his or her experience.

Alternatively – or additionally – consider offering a money-back guarantee if for any reason your client isn't satisfied with your services.

In an old adage, two men wanted to sell their horses. The first one merely showed the horse to possible buyers, while the other told the first prospect to take the horse with him (along with the food for the horse – bought by the owner), ride it for a week and then either pay for it or take it back to the owner – no hard feelings. Guess who sold the horse first.

If you already have experience as a freelancer but still struggle to get more jobs, consider setting up your own website and differentiating yourself among others by adding a content part to your site – articles about your profession, services, and information your clients would find useful. With a consistent writing schedule, your articles will get naturally attract eyeballs – and possible new clients.

There's much more you can do to find more time as a freelancer if you spend countless hours looking for more work. It starts with acknowledging the problem and looking for a more efficient way to handle it, though.

2. You have too many clients, but don't want to turn them down

If you're an established freelancer who enjoys plenty of word-of-mouth marketing, it's possible you're drowning in work – but you can't get yourself to refuse it and catch a breather.

The most obvious solution – and for many, the scariest one – is to raise your rates. While this move will deter some of the clients from using your services, it will give you some breathing room and ultimately, secure the high-quality of your services.

Moreover, higher prices signal higher value, and that makes it easy to attract solid, low-maintenance clients while keeping the most difficult ones away.

As a rule of thumb, clients who primarily look for a low price are a pain to deal with, while less price-sensitive clients cause few problems. Consequently, it's a yet another benefit that will help you save more time and headaches – while making more money.

Note that in an unlikely scenario of you increasing your prices and getting much fewer jobs than before, you can always revert to your previous prices. The risk is worth taking, because you have virtually nothing to lose, and plenty to gain.

3. You refuse to get help

Some freelancing jobs require your full focus, but some can be partly outsourced to help you focus on the most essential part of the job.

For instance, if you offer marketing services as a freelancer, it doesn't have to be you who's performing all of the marketing activities like researching potential advertising opportunities, creating new banners, analyzing data, etc.

Outsourcing even one part of the job – say, creating new banners – will free up your time to focus on the more valuable tasks that directly put the money on your table.

Oh, you're saying it will cost you to hire someone? It will, but you can spend additional time and energy on getting more jobs or just relaxing, thus optimizing your daily schedule as you wish.

Delegating certain tasks as a freelancer is simply a balancing tool that can help you balance between earning more money and having more time – without sacrificing the quality of your services.

If you've been a freelancer for some time and are ready to gain even more freedom – possibly at the expense of some initial growing pains – consider transforming your one-man operation into an agency. Speaking of which…

Scenario #3: Your Own Business
Gives You the Most Freedom

Last but most definitely not least, the route that allows the most freedom is entrepreneurship – the ultimate way to build not only time, but also financial freedom.

As an owner of a company, you only report to yourself. While the job comes with both perks and drawbacks, in the end it's the only position that lets you completely control your schedule.

When you think of the word "entrepreneur," you may think of a boss, a manager, or simply a person who has the entire company on his shoulders and is even more chained to the job than a regular employee.

However, while you can optimize this approach and make it work, too, an alternative opportunity I'm a big fan of is the growing trend of "solopreneurship."

Solopreneurial ventures are usually tiny businesses owned by just one person. They're tiny, but since all of the money goes directly to the owner, they can be more lucrative than million-dollar companies with dozens of people on the payroll and a board of investors.

If a solopreneur has any employees, they're all contractors and other temporary workers who provide their services on a flexible basis, thus requiring much less management time than a regular 9 to 5 employee.

According to the 2015 MBO State of Independence Survey, almost three million Americans reported annual earnings of $100,000 or more in their solo businesses[17]. It's a 45% increase since 2011. These numbers include both traditional freelancers offering services as well as one-man businesses selling products or services.

In today's well-connected world, you no longer have to run a huge corporation to achieve financial success as an entrepreneur. In fact, it's probably much easier and faster to do so with a tiny business than with a huge one.

Forbes.com contributor Elaine Pofeldt has covered numerous solopreneurs in her articles at Forbes.com[18]. Individuals covered in her article include an entrepreneur who has built a million-dollar business on small investments in local real estate[19], a young couple who created a $1 million-plus artisanal food business[20], and a man who left his project management career to start a seven-figure, one-person business selling planners[21], among others.

It's clear there's a lot of opportunity for people willing to go on their own. And fortunately, there are a lot of resources that can help you achieve this goal, too.

Some books that will help you learn more about how to become an entrepreneur in today's era of growing one-man flexible businesses include MJ DeMarco's *The Millionaire Fastlane* and Tim Ferriss' *The 4-Hour Workweek*.

If You're Already an Entrepreneur and Can't Find Time

Shark Tank's Lori Greiner once famously said that entrepreneurs are the only people who work 80 hour weeks to avoid working 40 hour weeks. Well, some do, but it's not because there's so much work to do – it's because they don't know how to manage their time and energy.

If Elon Musk, probably the most influential entrepreneur of our times, has the time to be a CEO of two billion dollar companies (Tesla Motors and SpaceX) and be a parent to his 6 kids, you can surely have the time for one tiny (in comparison to his ventures) business.

There are five keys to achieving more balance in your entrepreneurial life, based on my personal experience as well as the experience from other entrepreneurs I've got to know over the years:

1. The right business

Not all businesses will give you ultimate freedom over your schedule. A brick and mortar store – even if operated by your employees – will most likely always require your personal attention unless you hire a manager.

Almost all kinds of B&M businesses are time-consuming, but some online ventures can also work in a similar way if you cater to a group of people who can only buy your products during a specific period of time.

I had a business that offered software tailored to a certain group of business clients. However, it wasn't even half as flexible as a simple freelance job, because I had to fit my schedule around the business hours of my clients.

This meant that the bulk of my work could only be done between 9 AM and 5 PM during the week, a solution I found inflexible. It was when I closed this business and transitioned to another online business model that didn't require me to work specific hours that I regained control over my schedule.

Last but not least, as brutal as it sounds, each new hired employee robs you of personal time. Ideal businesses for people who want to enjoy a lot of time freedom are solopreneurial ventures that can be almost completely operated by other companies (Amazon's Fulfillment by Amazon program being one example), software, or that don't require customer support.

If you own a restaurant, a retail store or virtually any other kind of a local enterprise and you're strapped for time because you perform the role of the manager, chances are the situation won't change much over the years – unless you find a manager to replace you or sell the business and reinvest the earnings into something more flexible.

If you can, find a way to automate your business or delegate parts of the tasks to another company (let its managers spend time managing their employees while you enjoy free time).

As an author publishing my books on Amazon and other online retail stores, I have thousands of people working for me. My physical books are sent by one company. My ebooks are delivered through Amazon's or other retailers' servers. Payments, returns, and all other issues are handled by other companies. True, they take their cut for these services, but in exchange my workweek is much shorter.

2. Your one thing

Gary Keller is one of the most successful real estate entrepreneurs in the world. He has co-founded Keller Williams Realty, currently the largest real estate franchise by agent count in North America.

In his book *The ONE Thing: The Surprisingly Simple Truth Behind Extraordinary Results* he shares a simple strategy to tremendously improve your effectiveness while working much less. The idea is simple: you ask yourself what's the one thing you can do such that by doing it everything else will be easier or unnecessary. The book delves deep into how exactly to do it.

Ever since I've read Keller's book, I've been following his advice religiously. It has helped me gain more control over my time and increase my effectiveness by spending much less energy than before.

I identify my one thing in every single activity I do (both in business and personal life) and focus on it – while ignoring the less important things, either completely or doing them only when they finally become necessary.

For instance, as an author, whenever I write a new book, I don't obsess over the proper choice of words or grammar when writing my first draft. My one thing as an author is to write the first draft.

I don't spend my days fixing every little sentence, posting on social media, or designing covers for my books. My one thing is writing. One to two hours of focused writing a day brings me incomparably better results than spreading myself thin over many activities.

In one of my previous businesses (profitable since the first month) I followed the same strategy by doubling down on the most effective marketing techniques and ignoring the remaining ones.

The key to making the most out of identifying and performing your One Thing is to do it first thing in the morning. I usually have my One Thing done by 11 AM. Even if I don't do anything else later during the day, I still consider it a day of productive work. It gives me great peace of mind to know that by 11 AM I've achieved more than most people do during the entire 8-hour day of work.

How can you apply it to your situation? You can start with making a list of the most crucial activities in your business and then asking yourself which activities are the most profitable and most necessary for you. Ideally, it should be just one activity – not numerous activities.

Keep in mind, though, that the idea is to find one extraordinary thing that can make all of the other tasks unnecessary or easier. It's not merely about prioritization, but smart thinking.

When I write my books and make sure the final product is of as high-quality as I can make it, it makes it unnecessary to spend hours and hours on marketing – my content defends itself. Little marketing goes a long way if you first make sure you have a product worthy marketing.

When Gary Keller had a goal to grow his real estate agency, he didn't make it his goal to spend the first hours of the day talking with new agents or discussing new marketing techniques. Instead, he came up with an idea to write a bestselling book. His book has made him a well-known expert and attracted hundreds of new agents to join his company. His One Thing was successful because it rendered all other activities unnecessary or easier.

3. Delegation

Many entrepreneurs believe that the world will stop spinning if they're not around. This misguided belief causes them to spend unnecessary time doing things other people could do just as well, if not better.

When I stopped thinking I could do everything best and recognized that other people have other talents they can employ to generate better results than my mediocre attempts, my life got much easier.

For instance, in the past I spent hours trying to design good-looking covers for some of my (embarrassing) fiction stories. I could have just spent a few dozen bucks and got a slick and shiny cover made by a professional designer.

Even the excuse of not having money doesn't work here. If you have no idea how to design a professional cover but you try to do so anyway, the only result will be a mediocre cover that will decrease your sales. In other words, you save $50 on professional cover design to potentially lose thousands of sales.

Delegation is particularly difficult for control freaks who would like to control every aspect of their business. The more your business grows, the more parts it usually has. Hence, the more time you need to invest into controlling it, and the more busy you become. Delegation solves this problem – you just need to break through the resistance, let go of control, and trust that others will do just as well.

4. Passivity

Passive income is probably one of the most commonly mentioned terms online, particularly on numerous business forums. And while 100% passive income doesn't exist, some types of businesses are more passive than others.

As mentioned before, a brick and mortar store doesn't give you much freedom. As long as you remain the manager of the business, the business won't be passive – unlike, say, a business selling e-books for teachers or in the offline realm, an investor leasing his farmland.

We've already covered how Amazon and other retailers help me spend very little time on my self-publishing business. Amazon's

28

Fulfillment program works in the same way for physical products. Udemy is for video courses, ThemeForest is for website templates, iTunes App Store or Google Play App Store is for apps. All of these platforms make it easier to reach a huge base of clients as well as manage numerous time-consuming aspects of the business.

Most businesses can also become much more passive with a simple addition of a product sold for a recurring fee. As an example, a person who wants to start a website needs to buy hosting. Since the service is recurring by nature, the fee is recurring, too (usually monthly). A business becomes much more passive and less time-consuming if you know that each new client doesn't mean just $20 today, but $20 today, $20 in a month, another $20 in two months, and so on.

Putting more focus on the existing clients and marketing more to them rather than trying to attract new clients also makes it easier to increase the passivity of a business. Marketing is the most costly (both in terms of money and time) activity. If your venture can rely on repeat business (and it should), the needs and wants of your loyal clients are almost like free money lying on the table just waiting for you to pick it up.

Jay Abraham's *Getting Everything You Can Out of All You've Got* is possibly the best book on proven evergreen marketing strategies, many of which require little time because they focus on leveraging what you already have.

5. Products, not services

The final point partly goes back to the first point (choosing the right business), though there's a subtle difference between them.

Service businesses – including online businesses, are more difficult to turn into well-oiled machines than businesses selling products.

If you only sell services, you'll never escape the time-consuming problem of scaling your business. A service requires employees, and employees require management. The more clients you have, the more employees you need. Each new employee requires time-consuming training, made more difficult because of the fact that performing services isn't as predictable as shipping a product. Additionally, each new job requires creating a proposal, estimating a quote, etc.

A service-based business can be turned into more of a product-based business by packaging your service and marketing it as a product. For instance, a graphic design agency can offer three packages – a $100 option, a $250 option, and a $500, all with clearly defined features.

It greatly simplifies the business and allows more scale because it relies on repeatable, predictable processes. Customization is what makes the business more complex, and as a result more time-consuming to manage. You can learn more about Product as a Service business in Dan Norris' *The 7 Day Startup: You Don't Learn Until You Launch*.

If you have a product-based business, usually you can operate it completely alone or with just a small team. It makes it the best solution for people who prioritize time.

No matter if you sell 100 products, 500 products, 1000 products, or 10,000 products, your time investment can still be the same given that you use the services of a fulfilling company and have a virtual assistant (or two) to take care of customer support.

You Can Handle Your Biggest Time Suck

Even if your job currently takes the majority of your time, it doesn't mean it has to be like that for the rest of your life. A conscious choice of prioritizing time in your life will help you make the choices that will lead you to more freedom.

All you have to do is open up to the idea that you can multiply your output by minimizing your input in an intelligent way. Freelancing is the first step toward this goal, and entrepreneurship is the ultimate way to structure your life as you wish.

If you're sure you're not cut out to be your own boss, at least find a way to optimize your work life by becoming more effective at work, ideally getting a more flexible job that will allow you to reap more benefits from your improved productivity.

YOUR BIGGEST TIME SUCK: QUICK RECAP

1. A 9 to 5 job with fixed hours is your biggest time suck. There are several ways to gain more time or energy with such a job, but it will always be a suboptimal form of employment if you're looking for more time.

2. If you're not interested in looking for an alternative form of employment that allows setting your own hours, you can consider optimizing your effectiveness by taking breaks more often. As a result, you'll have more energy after work – and that will considerably increase the quality of your life.

3. Another option to optimize your traditional 9 to 5 job is to ask your boss if you may telecommute. Even if it's just a day or two a week without having to commute, it's still at least an hour or two a week for you.

4. If you want to have more freedom over your schedule but don't want to work for yourself, consider finding a more flexible job. Many jobs – primarily in sales and IT – can be done remotely, or at least flexible enough to move your daily schedule by an hour or two.

5. Becoming a freelancer is an even better idea to gain more control over your time. As a freelancer, you get three benefits that can help you save a lot of time:

Firstly, if you choose a completely remote freelance job, you no longer have to commute. In a big city, commuting can take up to 2 hours both ways. Getting rid of it results in an additional 10 hours a week of free time.

Secondly, being a freelancer gives you complete freedom over your schedule. If you have a project to be done by Friday, it doesn't matter if you do it Tuesday morning or at 2 AM on Thursday. What matters is the result, not when you work on it. Fitting work around your personal schedule and preferences – even if you work the same amount of hours – can make a huge difference to your levels of energy.

Thirdly, as a freelancer, you don't have to do everything by yourself. While your boss probably wouldn't appreciate you hiring external workers to perform some parts of your job, you can (and should) afford the luxury if you're your own boss.

6. The three most common reasons why freelancers don't have time are: struggling to get new jobs, getting too many jobs, and refusing to delegate certain tasks. By mastering the fundamentals of marketing, raising your prices, and delegating the less important parts of your job, you can have more time as a freelancer.

7. Entrepreneurship is the ultimate way to gain freedom over your schedule. Due to a growing trend of solopreneurship, you can start a small profitable company that won't require as much time as traditional, huge ventures with dozens of employees, managers, and investors.

8. If you're an entrepreneur and you're strapped for time, chances are it's because you've chosen the wrong business. In general, brick and mortar businesses and all kinds of businesses requiring people are more time-consuming than online, automated, or outsourced ventures.

9. An extremely powerful way to gain more time is to find the one thing you can do which will make doing everything else easier or unnecessary. The fewer tasks you have on your to-do list, the more effective you get –thus, you make more money while having much more time.

10. Delegation is one of the keys to regain control over your time as an entrepreneur. The more you can delegate to other people – ideally other companies or contractors and not employees – the more time you'll have for more important tasks.

11. Some types of businesses are more passive than others. Launching a business on a recognized platform with a huge client base – like Amazon – makes it much easier to spread the word about your products. Additionally, consider adding a product sold for a recurring fee and don't forget that a list of repeat buyers is an entrepreneur's goldmine. It's immensely less time-consuming to sell to your past customers than to find new ones.

12. Selling products is less time-consuming than selling services because it's easier to outsource it, and the process is simple to learn. If you sell services, consider packaging them as a product with specific features and a fixed price so you don't have to spend time giving quotes and preparing proposals.

Chapter 2: A Silent Robber of Your Time

A Microsoft study found that every time employees were interrupted by emails, phone calls, or messages, they needed an average of 15 minutes to return to their important projects[22].

It wasn't that they needed 15 minutes to deal with the interruption. The interruption in itself led to other distractions like surfing the web or spending time at social media sites.

Most of us get distracted at least a few times each day, so we probably lose up to a couple of hours a day on pretending to get things done. And that's just at work. Distractions in your personal life can lead to even worse problems, such as your spouse thinking you don't care about him or her, your kids feeling ignored, or you being unable to notice and enjoy the little – but important – things in life.

Distractions lower the quality of your life and steal your time under the pretense of doing something "urgent," but rarely important.

It's unlikely you'll ever achieve a 100% distraction-free lifestyle unless you decide to live in an isolation tank. However, with the right attitude and knowledge about distractions you can become more focused, effective, and consequently have more time.

Close the Door

Stephen King writes in his memoir and book on the craft of writing, *On Writing*, that the space in which you write "really needs only one thing: a door which you are willing to shut."

The closed door is both literal and figurative. A closed door signals to the external world that you're busy. However, even a bulletproof bank vault door won't help you handle distractions if you forget to close the other door – the one in your head constantly letting in random thoughts.

I'd be the last person to tell you that you can achieve a distraction-free lifestyle. Except for a handful of the most experienced Buddhist monks, I don't think anyone can work for hours on end without any distractions.

Since you can't eliminate them, learn how to manage them. One technique that provides a powerful solution is the Pomodoro Technique developed by productivity consultant Francesco Cirillo in the late 1980s[23].

Instead of trying to fight distractions, you schedule them to happen during a short, 3 to 5 minute break after a focused, 25 minute bout of work. After completing four pomodoros, you take a longer, 15-30 minutes break before going back to another set of pomodoros with shorter breaks.

If you get distracted during your 25-minute period of work, you log the distraction and act on it during your break. The door is closed while you work – and wide open while you take a break.

The technique has been used worldwide, and the book describing the technique in more detail has sold over 2 million copies. I've been personally using this technique while writing all my books. Short periods of focused writing have enabled me to increase my writing speed by at least 100% when compared to writing without breaking my sessions into periods of work and break.

Moreover, the Pomodoro Technique helps overcome procrastination. You probably wasted numerous hours distracting yourself to avoid getting to work.

Since one Pomodoro only takes 25 minutes, it greatly reduces the resistance to start working. After all, it's just 25 minutes, and after that, you get a 5-minute break. It usually takes only one or two Pomodoros to get into the flow and get rid of the temptation to keep procrastinating.

If you still find it difficult to start – even if it's just a period of 25 minutes of work – tell yourself you'll only do a given activity for a minute or two. That's how I begin my writing sessions on the days I find it hard to start. After the first 100 words I pick up momentum and the remaining 20+ minutes pass by quickly. Before I know it, my writing session is over – and I've saved time I would otherwise waste procrastinating.

You can use the same approach to handle distractions in your personal life. If you often find yourself glued to your smartphone, tell yourself that, for the next 25 minutes, you'll give your full attention to the world around you. After 25 minutes, you have 5 minutes to check your phone and do whatever you want.

By setting aside time for distractions – and resisting them until your break is due – you free up your focus during the periods you need it, and that, in itself, is an effective practice at becoming a more mindful person.

A Powerful Exercise to
Handle Distractions Better

In some of my previous books, and primarily *Daily Self-Discipline*, I cover the topic of meditation and how powerful it is for both self-discipline as well as learning how to deal with distractions. I won't repeat this advice here, but instead give you another powerful exercise that will help you learn to handle distractions better.

The revolutionary idea is to... take up a sport.

You can't get good at a sport if you don't learn how to focus. Sports you find enjoyable will make it easy to forget about your problems and the world around you and immerse yourself in the experience.

I'm partial to climbing and tennis – two sports that require a huge dose of concentration to perform them properly. The meditative experience of balancing on a wall or following a small yellow ball with your eyes helps me develop "tunnel vision mode" I can then use in other areas of my life.

Other good sports that will help you develop more focus and resist distractions include: chess, archery, martial arts, gymnastics, golf, snooker, and skiing. Every sport that requires precision, accuracy, and quick reaction time will be helpful at improving your focus.

The consistent, regular practice will result in a multitude of additional benefits, some of which – besides learning how to focus – will also help you have more time.

Enter the Flow

Hungarian psychologist Mihaly Csikszentmihalyi describes in his book, *Flow: The Psychology of Optimal Experience*, the theory of *flow*, the feeling of being in the zone in which you forget about the world around you and get completely immersed in the experience.

Flow is the state of hyperfocus in which the only thing that matters is the activity you perform. Everything else – the concept of time, self, hunger or thirst, etc. fades into the background.

While hyperfocus can sometimes be bad – think people dying after playing video games for three days in a row without any breaks – flow is generally a good thing as long as you don't go overboard with it (and hey, even too much salt or water can kill you).

Sports are one example of being in the flow state. All of the world's most successful professional players get into the zone on a regular basis. Other activities in which flow can play a huge role (and that can train you to become better at handling distractions) are:

- education – including self-learning. Acquiring new skills, challenging yourself, and achieving results will all help develop a better ability to focus.

- music – you can enter the state of flow when playing an instrument – particularly when you already play it well. Improvisational soloists –pianists[24], for instance – can enter the state of flow most easily.

- social settings – if you've ever felt it was just you and your interlocutor, you were in the state of flow. The same can happen during public speaking and all other kinds of social interactions that require focus.

- work – and that's where the concept of flow is the most useful for our topic of discussion. The better you are at entering the zone, the better you'll get at resisting distractions and the more effective you'll become. As a result, you'll have more time for other tasks – or more time to do something that isn't work-related.

The most important conditions for entering the zone when working are:

1. You must have a clear goal. If you don't know what you need to achieve, your mind will wander.

2. You must receive clear and immediate feedback or results. If you can't tell whether the action you're performing is effective or not, you won't sustain the feeling of flow.

3. You must be confident in your abilities to complete the task you're performing. If you think the activity you want to perform is beyond your skills, you'll enter the state of frustration, definitely not flow. However, the task shouldn't be too easy or you'll get bored. Ideally, the activity you perform should stretch your abilities.

When I write this book, I have a clear goal of writing 1500 words a day. I immediately get results in the form of new paragraphs as I see the words appear on the page. As an additional way to get myself in the zone, I set short deadlines.

At the time I'm writing these words, I have an hour left to leave for my tennis class. I still have almost 1000 words left to write and I'm confident they'll appear on these pages before I leave. If I didn't have such a short deadline – and instead told myself I can finish the remaining words once I get back home – I would probably write more slowly and with less focus.

Steven Kotler, bestselling author of *The Rise of Superman: Decoding the Science of Ultimate Human Performance*, says in his article for FastCompany.com that taking risks drives focus into the now and helps achieve the state of flow[25].

As he notes, "Move fast and break things. Engage in rapid experimentation. High consequences will drive flow and you get farther faster."

Increasing the stakes and moving faster – even if it's something as small as a short deadline – will tremendously improve your effectiveness, and thus let you find more time for other activities in life.

There's no limit to the opportunities in which you can use flow. If you make it a conscious choice to get in the zone for all of the important tasks in your life instead of half-assing things, you'll become much more effective.

I don't know about you, but I will always choose an hour of deeply focused, intense work over three hours of weak efforts interrupted by distractions.

An additional benefit of being in the zone is that you focus on a single activity – and that's the ideal way to achieve maximum effectiveness. Multitasking has been proven to be a myth – our brain isn't capable of doing two things at once. It can only get better at creating the impression that it does two things at once – while processing one task at a time.

As the scientists from the Vanderbilt University note, "Our findings also suggest that, even after extensive practice, our brain does not really do two tasks at once. It is still processing one task at a time, but it does it so fast it gives us the illusion we are doing two tasks simultaneously"[26].

As behavioral psychologist Susan Weinschenk notes in her article on multitasking, "each task switch might waste only 1/10th of a second, but if you do a lot of switching in a day it can add up to a loss of 40% of your productivity"[27]. Additionally, it leads to making more errors.

The conclusion is simple – instead of dreaming about performing several tasks at once, learn how to get in the zone and stay there. Your brain will thank you – and you'll have much more time and energy to complete other tasks.

A SILENT ROBBER OF YOUR TIME:
QUICK RECAP

1. Even a brief interruption can lead to 15 minutes of lost time. A few distractions a day can steal up to a few hours of your productive time. Consequently, it's crucial to learn how to handle distractions better.

2. Closing the door – both literally and figuratively – will help you get better at developing focus. While you'll probably never eliminate all of the distractions from your life, you can learn how to manage them – and that will result in improved effectiveness and more time you can spend on something else.

A powerful way to do so is to use the Pomodoro Technique in which you work for 25 minutes and then take a short 3-5 minute break for any distractions you want. Such an approach helps you maintain focus while working on your task and lets you increase effectiveness for longer periods of time.

3. Taking up a sport is one of the best ways to learn how to improve your focus. The best sports to learn how to handle distractions better are sports that require precision, intense focus, and accuracy.

4. The state of flow is getting in the zone – being so immersed in the activity you perform that the world around you ceases to exist. As a result, you're hyper-focused, the distractions completely disappear, and you become hyper-effective.

5. You can enter the zone while performing a wide variety of activities in life: sports, playing music, education, being in a social setting, working. The more often you get in the zone, the better you become at handling the distractions. Consequently, you become more resistant to interruptions, and that alone can tremendously increase your effectiveness and help you have more time.

6. If you want to get in the zone while working, make sure you have a clear goal, an easy way to judge your effectiveness, and an activity that is not beyond your abilities but still slightly stretches them. An additional way to increase the chances of getting in the zone is to take risks or put more pressure on yourself: setting short deadlines for instance.

7. Your brain is not capable of multitasking. It can only switch between one task and another, which results in productivity decreasing by up to 40%, and making more errors.

Chapter 3: Why a Materialistic Lifestyle Is Too Time-Consuming (and What to Do About It)

The more you think you need, the more time-consuming your life is.

What the heck do I mean by that, and does it mean I want you to become a monk?

Not really.

In the following chapter we'll dig into the topic of materialism and how it entraps you and robs you of your precious personal time – usually for little to no reward.

Some people like to say that money doesn't bring happiness. I don't agree with that, but neither do I think that it's money in itself that makes you happy. It's *freedom* – and the wealth of options it provides.

A billionaire who's so busy he has neglected his family, alienating them until his wife and kids don't want to talk with him is not happy nor wealthy. He has money, but he doesn't have time, freedom, and loved ones with whom he can share the happiness.

Deceased British billionaire Felix Dennis wrote in his book *How to Get Rich* that "Up to just seven years ago I was still working twelve to sixteen hours a day making money. With hundreds of millions of dollars in assets I just could not let go. Like I said, it was pathetic. Because whoever dies with the most toys doesn't win. Real winners are people who know their limits and respect them."

Until he was 52, Felix Dennis had money (billions to be exact), but not wealth.

I once lived for a few months on a small tropical island in Mexico. Except for the delivery vans, there were no other cars on the island. All of the residents who could afford it used golf carts as their mode of transport. Those who couldn't had bikes or walked.

They weren't rich in the materialistic sense. They didn't drive expensive cars, live in huge villas, wear designer clothes, or go shopping to a huge shopping mall three times a week.

But they were happy. They had enough. Their families were nearby. They didn't have to spend hours in traffic jams. They worked in hospitality, were fishermen, or had small local businesses. None of them were forced to work in a soulless corporation in a small, dark cubicle enclosed by dozens of the same workplace stations.

They could afford to take a walk by the beach or have a picnic with their family. They could spend hours having dinner with friends. They could have a party and not worry about the next day of work.

I don't want you to think their lives were perfect or that you should pack your suitcases and fly there. I'm sure they had their share of problems. However, even if their bank accounts (if they had them) were empty, they still wore a smile on their face and had something most people living in the more "civilized" world don't have – time.

And that brings us to the purpose of this chapter – how you can become more like the residents of this Mexican island, even if you don't plan to ever leave your busy, bustling city. Let's start with a common problem that entraps so many people in a circle of busyness.

Keeping Up With Others Is Insane
for Your Wallet and Time

When we use the idiom "keeping up with the Joneses," we refer to benchmarking ourselves against our neighbors as a way to judge our social status or material status.

If your neighbor has an SUV for 6 people, you no longer want your compact sedan. If all of the people around you wear expensive designer clothes, you can't buy clothes second hand. If your colleague went to Fiji for vacation, your yearly trips to Hawaii, let alone Florida, are pitiful.

Of course, I'm exaggerating. Few people are so into keeping up with the Joneses that they do all of the aforementioned things. However, most of us do engage in the same practice one way or another. When we do it, though, we can act irrationally.

A study by researchers at the University of Warwick and Cardiff University has found that money only makes people happier if they make more than their friends and colleagues[28].

The fact that you're highly paid isn't enough – what is important is being better than others, or in other words, surpassing the Joneses.

A study conducted by Sara J. Solnick and David Hemenway in 1998 came to a similar conclusion[29]. The researchers found that people preferred to earn $50,000 a year while everyone else earned $25,000 instead of earning $100,000 themselves while others earned $200,000.

How crazy is that? We can get so into keeping up with others that we'd be happy to accept a $50,000 lower salary as long as others would make even less.

If you live a materialistic lifestyle and constantly compare yourself to others, chances are that you'll get dissatisfied the moment you can't keep up with them.

This discontentment will lead you to work even harder to make money (or borrow it) to keep up with others. As a result, you'll be even more enslaved than before – but you'd be (falsely) happy because you'd be just like your neighbors, including having little to no time for yourself and your family.

No other word but "insane" can describe this phenomenon. Its most visible effect is the level of personal debt in the US.

In 2015, an average indebted household had $15,762 in credit card debt, $27,141 in auto loan debt, $168,614 in mortgage debt, and $48,172 in student loan debt[30]. When we exclude mortgage debt and student loan debt (as they might not be related to the materialistic lifestyle), we're still left with over $40,000 in debt just because people keep up with the Joneses.

Living above one's means leads to debt, and debt needs to be repaid. And what do you need to repay the debt? You need to work more and more hours, suffering from a lack of time as well as causing suffering to your family and friends who can't spend time with you.

A materialistic lifestyle is also costly because of the side effects of having a lot of stuff. The more things you have, the more time and

48

money you'll spend maintaining them, storing them, replacing them, buying them, and so on.

I wrote an entire book about how to simplify your life and shift your focus from "to have" to "to be." It's called *Pure and Simple*, and it will serve as a valuable companion to this chapter. What I didn't discuss in that book, though, is how keeping up with the Joneses steals time and how you can put an end to it. As a short recap of *Pure and Simple* and to help you increase free time, let's discuss five steps to detach yourself from a materialistic lifestyle.

5 Steps to Stop Keeping Up with the Joneses

There are five crucial steps to take to stop keeping up with the Joneses and escape the vicious cycle of getting into more debt or working more for the sake of one-upping someone else.

1. Disassociate your self-worth from your status

The primary reason for the phenomenon of keeping up with the Joneses is that people tend to associate their self-worth with their status. You think it's your home, car, vacations, or clothes that define you, so if you lack something others have, you automatically feel bad about it – and want to fix it by buying what everyone else has.

Since others always want to be better than you, they keep buying more and more expensive things for the fleeting feeling of happiness that surpassing the Joneses provides. You in turn do the same. You don't want your ego to feel threatened, do you?

The moment you cease associating your self-worth with your status is the moment you break the bond that keeps you in the rat race.

This process can take a lot of soul searching and practice. If you've always defined yourself by the number of toys you have, don't expect to throw away all of them overnight and feel good about it.

Usually, associating self-worth with social status comes from the inability to recognize your inherent value as a human being. In other words, your self-esteem is conditional and dependent on something external. Ceasing to buy new toys can feel like losing a part of yourself.

Deriving your self-worth from what you have or how others perceive you is like being a guy who can pick up any girl in his Lamborghini but is unable to open his mouth when he's walking in his old sweatpants. His car defines his self-confidence, and he finds himself worthless without it. It's not a good position to be in, is it?

The most important way I've found to stop deriving your self-worth from your status is to focus on giving. The act of giving – and not necessarily in financial terms, but in terms of serving others as best as you can – lets you forget about your ego, shifts your focus to others, and consequently makes you feel good – while making the world around you a better place.

Altruism – just plain old effort to become the best person you can be for and towards others (and not buying the best car you can afford) – reduces stress, improves mental and physical well-being, and makes people feel a deeper connection to others[31].

All of these things will help you shift your focus from the consumer's belief of "who dies with the most toys wins" to the producer's "who helps the most wins" in which you stop caring about impressing others and no longer need to keep up with the Joneses.

More specific advice about building inherent self-esteem if the problem is rooted in your childhood is beyond the scope of this book. It requires deep psychological investigation a short subchapter in this book can't offer.

2. Go past the surface

It's easy to fall victim to thinking that everyone else's life is perfect and only yours is so bad. In reality, we're all similar to each other, but some people are better than others at hiding their struggles and their real lifestyles.

I play tennis in a place that primarily serves the "upper class" type of clientele. I often see expensive cars parked by the court – limousines, sports cars, huge SUVs – some of which are probably worth more than a small apartment in the city.

An "I need to keep up with the Joneses" person would start thinking how he, too, can park an expensive sports car there so his middle-class SUV or – God forbid – compact sedan wouldn't stick out like a sore thumb.

You could be tempted to think that all of the people who own these cars are extremely rich. Yet, many, if not most of those cars, are leased, and the owners could never afford to buy them in cash.

It's only an illusion of wealth. And it's costly, as the average lease for an expensive car can go well over $1000 a month. The need to create the image of success costs them money and time needed to be able to pay their monthly lease.

Each time you find yourself envious of somebody else's property, go past surface thinking. The people who have the flashiest cars and mansions are usually the ones who can't afford them.

3. Focus on what's important

If you occupy yourself with keeping up with others, it's possible you no longer know (or have ever known) what truly makes you happy.

Buying more and more toys has a way to make you forget that the only two things that truly matter in life for happiness are health and good people around you. True, physical possessions and experiences you can buy can make you happier, but without health, family, and friends, it all doesn't matter much.

A lonely billionaire left alone in his million-dollar mansion without his wife and children might be more comfortable than a poor person waiting out a storm in her shack, but he would most likely trade in a heartbeat to be surrounded by his family.

Chasing after the illusive image of success can not only rob you of money and time, but also personal happiness. Is it really worth it?

I'm not saying that you should stop seeking financial wealth. Life is better with money, but there's a difference in seeking meaning in financial wealth and building financial wealth to better enjoy what's truly important to you.

It was only after I spent over three months on that small Mexican island and came back home that I appreciated my friends and family more – and never again made the mistake of neglecting them, thinking I'd be happier traveling long-term as many people dream.

Take some time to ponder on what's important in your life and whether you spend enough time cultivating it. The next step will help you achieve that.

4. Trade expectation for appreciation

Elite performance coach Tony Robbins once said: "The day you trade expectation for appreciation is the day you become wealthy"[32].

Trading expectation for appreciation is the key to happiness and the highest form of wealth – contentment. What you achieve doesn't matter unless you learn how to appreciate it and cultivate it.

If you're unable to express your gratitude for the car you drive or the house in which you live, and instead complain you should be driving a Ferrari by now, you'll never find peace, and the rat race will never end for you. As a result, busyness for the sake of collecting more meaningless toys will rule your life.

Start today by expressing your gratitude for just a few things in your life and continue the practice every single day for the next three weeks.

I'm sure that after 21 days – if you commit to the process – you'll become much happier. You'll open your eyes to the fact that working so hard for the sake of keeping up with others makes no sense.

With appreciation, your current car or house will be good enough for you, and you'll refocus to find more time for other important things in life instead of chasing after more useless toys.

5. Acquire financial education

Instead of thinking of your money in terms of "how do I spend it?" think of it in terms of "how can I use it to increase my peace of mind?"

In the end, money is a tool for freedom and multiplying choices – whether it's the freedom to work fewer hours, switching your career, or just being able to spend more time with your family instead of in your office.

An emergency fund – keeping cash to cover all of your expenses for at least three months – is the most basic and most important concept in personal finance.

Responsible financial behaviors will help you build a nest egg that will allow you to prioritize time investment over financial investment. Money in itself won't make you happy, but the choices it provides – like being able to take a few weeks off to take your family for a long vacation or just work fewer hours during the week – will.

Don't make the same mistake as 62% of Americans who have less than $1,000 in their savings accounts[33], having essentially no opportunities to optimize their lives to be richer in time.

WHY A MATERIALISTIC LIFESTYLE IS TOO TIME-CONSUMING AND WHAT TO DO ABOUT IT): QUICK RECAP

1. People who are financially wealthy are not necessarily wealthy in terms of time and happiness. Oftentimes people who live simple and unglamorous lives are happier than the ones who have millions or billions because they're able to spend time doing something they like.

2. While it isn't practical or sensible to sell all of your belongings and move to a small tropical island, there's a lot you can gain from learning how to need less. As you renounce some of your most basic "needs" like an unnecessarily expensive car, a huge house, or designer clothes, you can get closer to the sweet spot of having both time and money.

3. People are happier when they make more than their friends and colleagues. If they could make much more than they do now – but less than others – they'd rather choose the status quo. This illogical phenomenon has its roots in keeping up with the Joneses and constantly using others as a benchmark for your social or financial status.

4. The more you live above your means, the less time you have and the more entrapped you become in the system where personal debt is so prevalent it's not even worth talking about. Putting an end to comparing yourself with others and no longer trying to one-up them will enable you to find out what you want in life and what you truly care about.

5. If you associate your self-worth with your status, you'll never be content. The race to get a better car, house, vacation, or clothes never ends – and it takes more time to deal with the extra debt and other obligations you collect along the way. Try to switch your attitude from the consumer's approach of "who dies with the most toys wins" to "who helps the most wins" to stop caring about impressing others.

6. Go past the surface when comparing yourself to others. Your neighbor who drives a Mercedes probably doesn't own it. He creates the image of wealth by leasing it, thus perhaps looking better in the eyes of the others at the expense of acquiring even more debt and losing even more time he now needs to spend to afford the car.

7. If you think in terms of "to have," it's easy to forget what's truly important in your life (and let me assure you, you won't ask people to fetch your Mercedes on your death bed). Ponder on what is valuable in your life and whether you spend adequate time doing it.

8. Gratitude is one of the keys to contentment. If you can trade expectation for appreciation, you'll gain more peace of mind and finally discover that what you have is enough – and that you really don't need to spend that much time and energy trying to get better and better things.

9. Savings brings peace of mind and gives you more options. You can do much more with $30,000 in your savings account – for instance, recharging your batteries with a week or two off with your family – than $30,000 spent on a new car that will require you working even more to afford it.

Chapter 4: Work Hard and Reap the Losses

There's a pervasive romantic notion that hard work is all that matters, and the harder you work, the more benefits you reap. Unfortunately, working hard in itself is likely to generate more losses than benefits.

I'm not saying that hard work is useless. What's useless is mindless hard work fueled by the myth that the harder you work, the better results you get. The question shouldn't be: "how can I work harder?" but "how can I work smarter?"

You can only increase your output so much by working harder. We all have limited time and energy, so there's a limit to how hard you can work before you pass out. However, there's no limit to human ingenuity and intelligence – and that's the only route that will allow you to achieve more while working less.

In this chapter, we'll explore how you can switch from thinking in terms of "hard work" to "smart work" – work that you can optimize to such an extent that it will go from feeling like drudgery to feeling almost too easy.

Please note that I use the word "work" to describe all kinds of tasks you do to achieve a specific goal, not necessarily work in terms of your career or business. In other words, it can be working to make money, working to learn a skill, working to become a better performer, etc.

You Already Know This Rule

And you most likely don't believe it, or you follow it rarely.

I'm talking about the 80/20 Rule, also known as the Pareto Principle that states that 80% of the output (money, results) comes from 20% of the input (effort, time).

We've already covered in Chapter 1 that finding your One Thing can help you achieve much better results in much less time. The 80/20 Principle is the basis for this concept. Bestselling author Richard Koch's question in his book *Living the 80/20*, "What will give me a much better result for a lot less energy?" has different wording, but the same meaning behind it.

Abraham Lincoln once said: "Give me six hours to chop down a tree and I will spend the first four sharpening the axe."

If you take the time to figure out how you can make your job easier, you'll become more effective than a person who simply works as hard as she can. As a result, you'll finish your task more quickly, while exerting less energy.

As we've also already discussed in Chapter 1, your possibilities to save a lot of time when working are better when you work on your own.

If you work for somebody else, multiplying your output won't mean you'll be able to lessen your work to 10 hours a week. That's why it's so crucial to either find a job that is more flexible and dependent on the results you generate or to become your own boss.

However, you can follow the same rule in other areas of your life to reduce the time spent on some activities and still get the same – or better – results than before.

For instance, you can apply the rule in education.

A Florida State University study on top musicians, athletes, actors, and chess players shows that elite performers don't work harder. Their sessions are usually no longer than 90 minutes. The difference, though, is that their sessions are highly focused[34]. They also rarely practice for more than four and a half hours a day. They work smart instead of working hard – and that's precisely why they're elite performers.

As researcher Dr. Ericsson says, "To maximize gains from long-term practice, individuals must avoid exhaustion and must limit practice to an amount from which they can completely recover on a daily or weekly basis."

Which leads us to the second important point:

Exhaustion Isn't Effective

Sleep deprivation is often worn as a badge of honor. "I'm so busy I don't have time to sleep. Look at me, I'm so important!"

According to the CDC, 35.5% of Americans sleep less than 7 hours during a typical 24-hour period[35]. According to data from the National Health Interview Survey, nearly 30% of adults reported an average of less than 6 hours of sleep per day in 2005–2007[36].

If an average adult needs about 7–8 hours a day of sleep, getting slightly less surely isn't going to affect her much, right?

Unfortunately, that's not the case.

A 2003 study on sleep deprivation showed that chronic restriction of sleep to 6 hours or less per night produced the same cognitive performance deficits as going without sleep for two nights straight[37].

Here's where things get even worse: the group that slept for 6 hours per night for two weeks didn't rate their sleepiness as being as bad as people who went without sleep for two nights straight – even though the cognitive performance was just as bad. They weren't aware of their decreasing cognitive performance despite being on exactly the same level as the people not sleeping for two days.

And if things weren't already bad, a 2008 study on sleep duration shows that, on average, people overestimate the amount of sleep they're getting by 48 minutes[38]. In other words, if you think you're getting 7 hours of sleep a night, it's possible you actually get just a little over 6 hours and you're in the area of chronic sleep deprivation.

The CDC reports that the most common self-reported sleep-related difficulties among adults over 20 years in from 2005 to 2008 are visible when:

- concentrating on things (reported by 23.2% of people)

- remembering things (reported by 18.2% of people)

- working on hobbies (reported by 13.3% of people)

- driving or taking public transportation (reported by 11.3% of people)

- taking care of financial affairs (reported by 10.5% of people)

- performing employed or volunteer work (reported by 8.6% of people)

60

Sleeping fewer hours so you have more time is an illusion of a good investment. You think you save one or two hours each night, but in reality you trade one or two hours of recharging sleep for the entire day of decreased performance. Where's the return on investment here?

Vacations also play an important role in increasing productivity and work in the same way as getting adequate sleep. What you think you save when you don't take any time off during the year actually results in decreased long-term performance. Gaining a fresh perspective by going on a vacation can save you weeks or months of work.

Americans are among the worst nations when it comes to taking time off. According to Expedia's 2015 Vacation Deprivation Study, Americans get an average of 15 days off each year and take only 11[39].

In comparison, workers in Germany, France, Italy, Spain, Sweden, Denmark, and Finland are all offered 30 days off. The Germans, French, Spanish, and Finnish lead by taking nearly all of those days, while the Danish take 28, and Italians and Swedes 25. In Brazil, workers also get 30 days off and they also use nearly all of them.

According to the study, 92% of Americans agree that they feel happier after a vacation. Yet, 53% of Americans feel they are "somewhat or very" vacation deprived.

In a study for Project: Time Off, conducted by the Society for Human Resource Management (SHRM), vacation positively impacts the workplace. 77% of HR managers agree that employees who take most or all of their vacation time are more productive in their jobs than those who do not[40].

Moreover, 75% of managers agree that using vacation time leads to higher performance, and 78% think it results in increased job satisfaction – all of which will result in more energy and time you otherwise waste on being overworked and less productive.

Taking time off might not necessarily be about refreshing your brain and subsequent improved productivity. The mechanism acts like the Pomodoros because going on a vacation means less time working during a given year, and that forces you to get more productive.

As leadership development consultants Jack Zenger and Joseph Folkman note in their article "Are We More Productive When We Have More Time Off?" for *Harvard Review*, "it's not that taking a break will refresh your brain and let you get more done; it's that simply spending less time at your desk forces you to waste less time"[41].

No matter the reason, taking time off *will*, in one way or another, help you become more productive, and that will result in more time and energy left for other things.

Don't Be a Martyr

Dr. Gilda Carle, a professor emerita at New York's Mercy College interviewed for Project: Time Off's All Work No Pay study said: "Whether balance for you is taking time off for a long time, going to a movie, or taking your kid to the zoo, no matter what you're doing or who you are, you must break your usual pattern"[42].

62

The report warns that people who don't use their time off are losing out on quality time with their significant other (85%), their children (85%), and themselves (81%). Moreover, the average person misses more than three personal events a year. 35% miss a child's activity. 25% miss out on vacations, 20% on visiting family, and 10% on funerals.

If you ask a regular person in the street whether work or family is more important, most wouldn't hesitate for even a second that their family is their priority. Yet, 43% of American workers spend less than 20 hours a week with their families. This means that an average American spends well over two times more time at work (50 hours) than at home with family.

As Dr. Gilda Carle notes, "The fear that is permeating the American workers who I have seen is pretty overwhelming. But they don't have the same fear of losing their spouse or their loved one. Isn't that interesting?"

Finding more time in your life isn't only about optimizing every single aspect of what you do. It's also about changing your mindset so you realize what's at stake when you choose to become a martyr at work.

Don't be the person who chooses work over a child's activity, and then regrets not spending enough time with her kid 20 years later. This book will help give you numerous ways to find more time, but you also have to change your mindset regarding taking time off and your priorities.

The data from the aforementioned study suggests that taking time off is the easiest way to avoid missing events. Over 60% of respondents said they never missed an event when they used their time off.

Don't be a martyr. The world won't crumble if you go on a vacation or attend your child's important event, like her first competition at school.

Once you optimize your sleep and vacation time – the two most important things that, when neglected, steal a lot of time and energy – we can proceed to optimizing your life by using the 80/20 principle in real-life situations.

Practical Ways in Which You Can Benefit from the 80/20 Principle

It can be difficult to come up with ways on how you can apply the 80/20 rule in your life, so below, I'll share with you some of the most common ways in which I follow the principle to tremendously reduce the time and energy I put into work to get better results.

1. Business

In my self-publishing business, at any given moment one or two titles account for the vast majority (over 90%) of my sales. I can look at the underperforming titles to avoid wasting time on writing books that people don't want to buy and spend more time writing books that people do want.

In every single business, there's always 20% (and usually less) of clients or products or marketing techniques that account for more than 80% of the sales. If you spend time identifying them and make an effort to focus most of your attention on these things, your revenue will soar – while the time you invest in your business will decrease.

I purposefully avoid spending time promoting my books on social media because the time invested in it won't justify the revenue it will bring.

Instead, I focus on the most important 20% (writing the best book possible and promoting it as heavily as possible during the first week) and disregard the rest. Consequently, I don't need to spend more than 10-15 hours a week on growing my business – and my results are better than the results of the authors who spend up to 12 hours a day writing and promoting their books without any primary focus.

You can apply the rule in a multitude of ways in your professional life. You don't even have to have a business to benefit from it. Just remember that 80% of what you produce will be the result of 20% of your efforts. Identify the 20% of your efforts and you're suddenly getting virtually the same results while spending five times less energy and time.

2. Learning foreign languages

Learning foreign languages takes much less time and energy when you follow the 80/20 rule and focus on the vital 20%.

In English, the most common 1,000 words account for 75% of the Oxford English Corpus, a collection of texts like books, newspapers, magazines, blogs, emails, speeches etc. that reflect the real-world spoken English[43].

In comparison, 7,000 most common words – six times the initial effort of learning 1000 words – account for 90% of the content.

By learning the 1,000 most common words first you'll understand 75% of the content. The remaining – six times bigger – effort will only result in understanding 20% more.

It doesn't mean it makes no sense to invest time in learning the remaining 6,000 words, though. The additional effort – even if it's six times more work than the first 1,000 words – can be worth it if you're after proficiency. If you're after basic fluency or want to learn as quickly as possible, starting with the 1,000 most common words is a great example of saving time by using the 80/20 principle.

If you've just started learning English, learning words like "crude," "tackle," or "purely" (out of the 7,000 most common words in English) won't be even half as useful as learning "girl," "win," or "difficult" (out of the 1,000 most common words).

3. Learning new skills

You can apply the same approach to learning new skills. All skills can be deconstructed to the most basic elements, out of which there's usually just one or two things that make all the difference.

For instance, in climbing – what most novices don't realize and consequently waste a lot of energy and time learning – is that the two most crucial skills to master are legwork (how to climb with your legs

66

rather than your hands) and keeping your arms straight (so you reduce the strength and stamina needed to climb by as much as possible).

If you focus on these two things right from the start – instead of wasting time training your forearms – you'll get better results more quickly than a person who doesn't learn in a smart way.

You can break down virtually every skill in a similar way and save energy and time on learning it. The key is to ask people – ideally elite performers – what's the most basic and most important thing you should learn, and dedicate yourself to it instead of spreading your attention over many, often more advanced, things.

4. Dealing with other people

You can apply the 80/20 principle even to such difficult to measure things as your social life. Generally speaking – and I'm aware how weird it sounds, but bear with me – 80% of your social enjoyment comes out of the 20% of the people you know.

If you currently complain you don't have enough time for everyone, ask yourself how much priority you give to people who matter a lot to you and how much time you spend with people you could live without.

Now ask yourself – is it worth it to spend your precious time with people you don't care much about? Reducing the time hanging out with people you don't consider your best friends – or eliminating it altogether – will result in more time for people you care about.

If 80% of your enjoyment comes from 20% of the people you know, then analogically, 80% of your dissatisfaction comes from 20%

of the people you know. Freeing yourself of these people will result in huge savings in time and energy without lowering the quality of your social life (and actually improving it).

I have a friend who, for a long time, was my best friend. Our paths diverged as he made some unambitious friends I couldn't stand.

I started spending less and less time with him and instead spent more time with other people who contributed to the quality of my life more. By doing this, I also eliminated a lot of drama. My friend was often late (so I wasted time waiting for him) and lacked initiative (so I wasted both time and mental energy to set up meetings).

I don't ask you to do a thorough 80/20 analysis of your friends and give them all a rating of enjoyment they provide you. The concept is about being more aware of who you hang out with and what the ratio is of how much time you spend with people you couldn't live without versus whom you could do without. Sometimes, for various reasons, these proportions can get out of whack, thus stealing away your time and energy.

5. Shopping

Few things frustrate me more than shopping, especially shopping for clothes. Consequently, I'm always eager to learn how I can make the experience less painful and finish it as quickly as possible.

My primary technique – derived from the 80/20 Principle – is to buy as few clothes as possible, but of as high-quality as reasonably possible (I won't buy a t-shirt for $200, but I won't buy it for $3, either). My reasoning is that according to the rule, 80% of the time I would only wear 20% of my clothes anyway.

By greatly limiting the number of clothes I have I avoid waste – both wasting money on clothes I wear rarely as well as time spent shopping. And since I wear the same pieces of clothing over and over again, a time-efficient option is to buy clothes of high-quality that won't wear out quickly, lessening wasted time having to buy replacements.

When you consider how much time and money you have to spend replacing cheap pieces of clothing every few months, it makes a lot of sense to pay more and avoid it. Don't also forget about the lower enjoyment you'll get out of cheap clothes as well as their general usefulness – if you don't *love* the clothes you buy, how often do you think you'll wear them when compared to a high-quality, timeless piece of clothing?

I also primarily shop online for everything I can, and that saves me hours I would otherwise have to spend on the nightmarish trip to a shopping mall. Such simple purchasing habits make my life easier and let me enjoy my free time rather than spend it doing something I dread.

WORK HARD AND REAP THE LOSSES:
QUICK RECAP

1. Working hard isn't optimal if your goal is to have more time. What you should focus on instead is working smart – improving your effectiveness in such a way that you can spend less time working, but still produce the same or better results than before.

2. The 80/20 Rule states that 80% of the outcome comes from 20% of the input. You can notice it working over and over again in all areas of life. Applying this rule to both your work and personal life will help you gain more time and energy while still getting great – if not better – results.

3. Exhaustion isn't effective. As obvious as it sounds, make sure you pay attention to how much you work and whether you take sufficient time off. Oftentimes working too much makes you blind to new ideas and perspectives because you're too exhausted to concentrate and end up doing the job by rote.

The most common problem with thinking that you can save time by working more is chronic sleep deprivation. It's a bad trade-off because you're "saving" one or two hours each night and getting lower performance that leads to taking more time to complete tasks, making more errors, and lowering your overall sense of well-being.

A related problem is working too much without taking any time off. Vacations can improve your productivity either by refreshing your mind and giving you a new perspective or by simply limiting the time you spend at work that consequently forces you to be more focused (in the same way as working in 25-minute sessions does). Letting yourself take a week or two off can result in increased productivity for months. Isn't that a good investment?

4. You can use the 80/20 principle in all walks of life.

In business, you can save time by identifying your most effective 20% and cutting away the rest.

In learning – such as new languages – focusing on the most common 1,000 words can lead you to basic fluency in a matter of weeks or months instead of years.

In your social life, spending more time with people who matter a lot to you and little (or no) time with people that aren't that important will result in more energy and often eliminate time-consuming drama from your life.

When shopping, you can save a lot of time by buying high-quality items. You need to replace low-quality products more often, you wear them less, and they give you less enjoyment. Paying a premium price results in saving time and getting higher satisfaction from your purchase.

Chapter 5: Structuring Your Lifestyle
for Time Maximization

In addition to time-maximizing techniques that you can apply in specific situations, there are a number of changes you can introduce in your daily life. In this chapter we'll discuss some of the most important factors that affect how much time you have or don't have each day.

Factor #1: When You Wake Up

If somebody told me just a couple of years ago to wake up early I would have shrugged and said it wasn't for me. For years, I was a night owl. I went to sleep around 3-4 AM and woke up well past noon.

At the time, I thought it was an optimal schedule as I enjoyed the quiet time at night. However, if you wake up at 1 PM, you don't have much sunlight left and the entire day feels extremely short.

Then I decided to experiment and started waking up around 6 AM. My days immediately became much longer. I maintain such a schedule to this day.

Now I have my most important tasks done by 11 AM or noon at the latest, and the rest of the day I can do whatever I want. I need to go to sleep much sooner to get at least 8 hours of sleep, but I'm not a partygoer anyway, so it doesn't matter.

Granted, as an entrepreneur, I have the luxury to set my own schedule, but even if you work from 9 to 5, waking up at 6 AM instead of, say, 7 or 7:30 gives you an additional hour of high energy you can use to do things for which you rarely have time later in the day.

Waking up early doesn't give you more time per se. It makes no difference if you go to sleep at 10 PM and wake up at 6 AM or if you go to sleep at 2 AM and wake up at 10 AM – you still sleep 8 hours. What waking up early accomplishes, though, is shifting your periods of high energy to earlier in the day.

Today, if I wake up at 10 AM instead of 6 AM, my days are shorter not because I wake up later, but because I now have to work on my most important tasks in the middle of the day when distractions break up my working sessions and reduce my effectiveness.

Even if you consider yourself a night owl, experiment with waking up early. I, too, believed that I would remain a night owl for the rest of my life. Today, I wake up earlier than most people I know.

Factor #2: Where You Live

There are two factors of where you live that affect how much time you have. Firstly, the location. If you live far away from your workplace or other places you visit frequently, you probably lose hours a week just on commuting alone.

I know a person who spends four hours a day commuting to another city. Okay, he might have a better salary than if he were to work in the city in which he lives, but at what cost? Is the increased salary worth what's essentially a part-time commute job?

You don't get paid for the time you spend commuting. If you added the commute time to the time spent at work, it's possible your hourly rate would drop by 20-30%.

Perhaps it would make sense to get a job that pays less, but frees up an additional several hours a week you can spend with your family?

The second factor of where you live is whether you live in an apartment or a house.

Generally speaking, a house will always require more maintenance than an apartment. The only occasional fixes you'll have to take care of in an apartment might be changing a lightbulb or replacing a filter.

If you live in a house, you need to set aside time for possible major repairs of the house itself (not your problem if you live in an apartment), landscaping – including everybody's favorite – lawn mowing (not your problem in an apartment), or snow shoveling (not your problem in an apartment).

Moreover, apartments are usually closer to the center of the city than houses. If you value having everything within your reach, living in an apartment might be a better choice than buying or renting a house in the suburbs where every single occasion to go out requires driving.

Granted, living in a house does offer some benefits an apartment doesn't. However, from the practical point of view – particularly for a single person – an apartment in which almost everything is taken care of for you is a better choice than a house.

Factor #3: How You Spend Your Free Time

What you do in your free time can affect how much time you have left for other things. Some activities are more time-consuming than others while not necessarily being good for you.

For instance, watching TV, one of the primary pastimes for many Americans, is a huge time-suck. According to the 2014 report from The Bureau of Labor Statistics, an average American spends 18% of his waking time watching TV – which is second to work with 23% of waking time and takes over twice more time than the next activity – eating and drinking (8%)[44].

While there's nothing wrong with watching some episodes of your favorite TV series a few times a week, channel surfing puts you in a zombie-like mindset of burning time like there's no tomorrow.

Other similar activities are using your smartphone, reading or watching the news, and surfing the Web. If you think you don't have much time, assess how many minutes (or most likely hours) you spend using the Internet, reading news, or on your smartphone in a mindless way. These four activities, when combined, can easily steal hours each day – and you won't even know what happened.

Factor #4: How and What You Eat

In my book, *Self-Disciplined Dieter*, I cover numerous techniques to help you improve your diet. Healthy eating will not only improve your health, but also improve your energy levels, and that will translate to better productivity and, in the end, more time for other things.

Unfortunately, many people opt out of healthy eating because they claim they don't have time to cook healthy foods. Just like not sleeping enough and not taking enough time off, eating whatever – just to save time – is another bad investment on your part.

Like I write in my book about dieting, if you don't make time for health, you'll have to make time for illness. And you're not just *running a risk* of falling ill. You *will* get ill if you continue eating unhealthy food. Hypertension, diabetes, heart disease, ulcers, back pain – all of these things can soon become (or perhaps already are) your daily companions.

There are three simple ways to save time in the kitchen:

- eating more frozen foods. They don't take much time to prepare as all you have to do is just steam and season them.

- cooking meals that keep for a few days. I have a habit of cooking soup every weekend. I cook it on Saturday and eat it for the next three days to get my daily fix of vegetables. There you go, problem of time-consuming cooking solved for three days.

- get someone else to cook for you. Eating out isn't optimal since you'll probably spend the same amount of time driving to a restaurant and waiting for your food to get delivered. However, you can consider using the services of a healthy meal delivery service (costly option), order healthy take-out (at least you don't have to waste time driving to get it), or perhaps get your roommate, friend, family member, or even a stranger to cook for you in exchange for money or help with something else.

I frequently mention in my books that I usually eat only one or two meals a day and then fast for the remaining hours. This nutritional habit has its own name – intermittent fasting.

I do it not only because of all the health benefits it provides (among others, beneficial effects on the cardiovascular and cerebrovascular systems[45], successful brain aging[46], better fat oxidation[47], reduced body weight, levels of bad cholesterol, LDL, and triglyceride levels[48]), but also because it gives me more time in the day.

In addition to intermittent fasting, I usually eat the same meals over and over again. I don't draw that much pleasure out of eating that I have to eat something new every single day, hence I optimize my eating habits in such a way.

Preparing three to five meals a day means:

- coming up with three to five ideas for meals

- prepping food three to five times (cleaning, cutting, slicing, cooking, etc.)

- washing dishes three to five times

I only have to do these things once, or at most, twice a day. And since I do it with the same meals over and over again, I have a system that helps me save time while doing it.

I don't believe it's the optimal approach for everyone. If it sounds strange to you, it probably isn't for you. If you're like me and eat primarily for fuel, it might work for you, though.

Factor #5: How Often and How You Exercise

In my book, *How to Build Self-Discipline to Exercise*, I talk about the deceptive savings you get when you choose not to exercise.

A simple calculation shows that investing just 22 minutes each day to exercise can most likely lead to at least one additional hour of productive time. Studies confirm that exercise increases productivity[49] and energy[50]. And that's just one benefit of exercise. Other benefits I also cited in the book include:

- a better ability to deal with stress, anxiety, and/or depression (exercise can alleviate symptoms among clinically depressed[51], reduce anxiety sensitivity[52] and treat depression and anxiety[53])

- feeling better about yourself (exercise improves self-worth in women[54], and is even more effective when done outdoors[55])

- stronger brainpower (exercise improves cognitive function in young adult males[56] and prevents cognitive decline that begins after age 45[57])

- improved creativity (exercise enhances creativity[58])

- better sleep (exercise improves sleep[59])

All these benefits, when combined, can lead to greatly increased productivity and energy, two of which will directly affect how much time you'll have left for other things in your life.

Exercise, sleep, and taking time off are all investments that might not look like a good idea if you're extremely busy. However, if you make sure not to neglect them, in the long term, you'll be able to sustain your work ethic for longer, make fewer mistakes, and get better results.

You can combine many types of exercise with other activities. For instance, if you like jogging, nothing prevents you from listening to an educational podcast at the same time. If you like riding a bike, you can get a friend to go with you. If you have to choose between spending time with family and exercise, why not take your family to the beach, for a walk in the park, or play Frisbee?

STRUCTURING YOUR LIFESTYLE FOR TIME MAXIMIZATION: QUICK RECAP

1. It's not only specific techniques that can help you save time during the day, it's also about structuring your life in such a way that it's optimized for more time. In addition to the things we've discussed in the previous chapters, there are five more important factors that affect how much time and energy you have: when you wake up, where you live, how you spend your free time, how and what you eat, and how often and how you exercise.

2. The time when you wake up can make a huge difference to your day. While sleeping for 8 hours between 10 PM and 6 AM or 2 AM and 10 AM doesn't change the fact that you still sleep 8 hours, waking up early gives you more hours of sunlight and lets you take care of the most important tasks before everyone, and everything, else, reducing distractions. Consequently, you won't have to worry in the middle of the day about the things you're yet have to do later in the day.

3. You can save a lot of time by choosing the right place to live. If you live far away from your workplace (or any other places you visit often), you lose a lot of time commuting. While you can more or less salvage time spent commuting by listening to educational audios, wouldn't it be better to be able to spend it at home or with your friends than in a traffic jam?

Another factor that influences how much time you have – or more specifically, how many obligations you have to deal with – is whether you live in a house or an apartment. Generally speaking, apartments are much less time-consuming than houses, particularly if you have a large backyard.

Living in a house provides benefits an apartment doesn't give, but for people strapped for time – especially young professionals – they might be worth forgoing in exchange for being close to everything (and not having to spend hours mowing the lawn or shoveling snow).

4. Mindless activities like watching TV, reading the news, surfing the Web and using your smartphone can all steal away a lot of free time without you even knowing what happened. Control how much time you spend in a mindless surfing state and ideally, limit it to a minimum.

5. Eating unhealthy food will sooner or later rob you of time and energy when you fall sick. It's not a question of "if," but "when." If you don't have time to eat healthy, eat more frozen foods (they're quick to prepare), cook for a few days (to save time on cooking), or get someone else to cook for you.

If the idea of eating one or two big meals a day interests you, consider experimenting with intermittent fasting. It can be a healthy way to further reduce the time you spend eating and cooking.

6. Exercise is not optional – it's mandatory if you want to stay a vibrant, healthy person. Saving time by not exercising doesn't result in saved time. It only leads to low energy that decreases your productivity, which consequently steals more time than investing at

least 20 minutes a day to exercise (producing high energy that gives you an edge over your tired self).

Epilogue

There's a famous Mark Twain quote I like to ponder on frequently: "Whenever you find yourself on the side of the majority, it is time to pause and reflect."

The ingenuity of these words is that you can apply them to virtually every single part of your life – including how busy you are.

Given the fact that most people complain about a lack of time, it's fair to say that if you follow what the others are doing, you'll end up in the same place and crave more free time as well.

If, however, you decide to take the path less traveled and introduce some or all of the unconventional ideas from this book, chances are you'll live a different life – for the better. All it takes is the guts to try and the brains to tweak the advice to fit your personal situation.

In today's world of tenfold, if not twenty- or thirty-fold more effective work due to computers, smartphones, the Internet, and numerous other modern inventions, time freedom is a choice. Unlike the poor farmer in the medieval times, you no longer have to slave away from sunup to sundown in the fields – unless you want to.

I invite you to commence the journey of cutting away the unessential in your life and improving your effectiveness. You can make more time and energy for the things that matter. Just give yourself a chance and make some changes.

Download Another Book for Free

I want to thank you for buying my book and offer you another book (just as valuable as this one): *Grit: How to Keep Going When You Want to Give Up*, completely free.

Visit the link below to receive it:

http://www.profoundselfimprovement.com/havemoretime

In *Grit*, I'll tell you exactly how to stick to your goals, using proven methods from peak performers and science.

In addition to getting *Grit*, you'll also have an opportunity to get my new books for free, enter giveaways, and receive other valuable emails from me.

Again, here's the link to sign up:

http://www.profoundselfimprovement.com/havemoretime

Could You Help?

I'd love to hear your opinion about my book. In the world of book publishing, there are few things more valuable than honest reviews from a wide variety of readers.

Your review will help other readers find out whether my book is for them. It will also help me reach more readers by increasing the visibility of my book.

About Martin Meadows

Martin Meadows is the pen name of an author who has dedicated his life to personal growth. He constantly reinvents himself by making drastic changes in his life.

Over the years, he has regularly fasted for over 40 hours, taught himself two foreign languages, lost over 30 pounds in 12 weeks, run several businesses in various industries, took ice-cold showers and baths, lived on a small tropical island in a foreign country for several months, and wrote a 400-page novel's worth of short stories in one month.

But self-torture is not his passion. Martin likes to test his boundaries to discover how far his comfort zone goes.

His findings (based both on his personal experience and on scientific studies) help him improve his life. If you're interested in pushing your limits and learning how to become the best version of yourself, you'll love Martin's works.

You can read his books here:

http://www.amazon.com/author/martinmeadows.

ISBN 978-83-952987-0-7

References

[1] Van Boven L., Gilovich T. (2003); "To Do or to Have? That Is the Question. " *Journal of Personality and Social Psychology* 85 (6): 1193–1202. DOI: 10.1037/0022-3514.85.6.1193.

[2] Van Boven L. (2005); "Experientialism, Materialism, and the Pursuit of Happiness." *Review of General Psychology* 9 (2): 132–142. DOI: 10.1037/1089-2680.9.2.132.

[3] Kumar A., Killingsworth M. A., Gilovich T. (2014); "Waiting for Merlot. Anticipatory Consumption of Experiential and Material Purchases." *Psychological Science* 25 (10): 1924–1931. DOI: 10.1177/0956797614546556.

[4] Pchelin P., Howell R. T. (2014); "The hidden cost of value-seeking: People do not accurately forecast the economic benefits of experiential purchases." *The Journal of Positive Psychology* 9 (4): 322–334. DOI: 10.1080/17439760.2014.898316.

[5] Department Of Psychiatry - Harvard Medical School - Research. Retrieved March 01, 2016, from http://www.hms.harvard.edu/psych/redbook/redbook-family-adult-01.htm.

[6] The "40-Hour" Workweek Is Actually Longer -- by Seven Hours. Retrieved March 04, 2016, from http://www.gallup.com/poll/175286/hour-workweek-actually-longer-seven-hours.aspx.

[7] Work and Workplace. Retrieved March 04, 2016, from http://www.gallup.com/poll/1720/work-work-place.aspx.

[8] Gifford, J. The Rule of 52 and 17: It's Random, But it Ups Your Productivity. Retrieved March 04, 2016, from https://www.themuse.com/advice/the-rule-of-52-and-17-its-random-but-it-ups-your-productivity

[9] Korkki, P. (2012). To Stay on Schedule, Take a Break. Retrieved March 04, 2016, from http://www.nytimes.com/2012/06/17/jobs/take-breaks-regularly-to-stay-on-schedule-workstation.html?_r=0

[10] In U.S., Telecommuting for Work Climbs to 37%. Retrieved March 04, 2016, from http://www.gallup.com/poll/184649/telecommuting-work-climbs.aspx

[11] 10 High-Paying Flexible Jobs. Retrieved March 04, 2016, from http://www.forbes.com/pictures/efkk45eeejm/10-high-paying-flexible-jobs/

[12] Parris, J. (2015). Most Flexible Careers for the Class of 2015 - FlexJobs. Retrieved March 04, 2016, from https://www.flexjobs.com/blog/post/most-flexible-careers-for-the-class-of-2015/

[13] Intuit 2020 Report: Twenty Trends That Will Shape the Next Decade. Retrieved March 07, 2016, from http://http-

download.intuit.com/http.intuit/CMO/intuit/futureofsmallbusiness/intuit_2020_repo
rt.pdf

[14] Freelancing in America: 2015. Retrieved March 08, 2016, from https://fu-web-
storage-prod.s3.amazonaws.com/content/filer_public/59/e7/59e70be1-5730-4db8-
919f-1d9b5024f939/survey_2015.pdf

[15] Table A-9. Selected employment indicators. Retrieved March 07, 2016, from
http://www.bls.gov/news.release/empsit.t09.htm

[16] Contently Study: The State of Freelancing in 2015. Retrieved March 07, 2016,
from http://contently.net/2015/06/22/resources/contently-study-state-freelancing-
2015/

[17] Mbo Partners State of Independence in America 2015. Retrieved March 08, 2016,
from https://www.mbopartners.com/uploads/files/state-of-independence-
reports/MBO-SOI-REPORT-FINAL-9-28-2015.pdf

[18] Elaine Pofeldt. Retrieved March 08, 2016, from
http://www.forbes.com/sites/elainepofeldt/

[19] Pofeldt, E. (2015, October 31). This Entrepreneur Built A Million-Dollar
Business On Small Investments In Local Real Estate. Retrieved March 08, 2016,
from http://www.forbes.com/sites/elainepofeldt/2015/10/31/he-went-from-earning-
50k-to-1-million-by-investing-in-local-real-estate/

[20] Pofeldt, E. (2015, August 30). Love And Honey: How A Young Couple Created
A $1 Million-Plus Artisanal Food Business. Retrieved March 08, 2016, from
http://www.forbes.com/sites/elainepofeldt/2015/08/30/this-1-million-plus-two-
person-business-runs-on-love-and-honey/

[21] Pofeldt, E. (2015, September 8). He Left His Project Management Career To Start
A Seven-Figure, One-Person Business. Retrieved March 08, 2016, from
http://www.forbes.com/sites/elainepofeldt/2015/09/08/he-left-his-project-
management-career-to-start-a-seven-figure-one-person-business

[22] Czerwinski, M., Horvitz, E., Wilhite, S.; "A Diary Study of Task Switching and
Interruptions." Retrieved March 09, 2016, from http://research.microsoft.com/en-
us/um/people/horvitz/taskdiary.pdf

[23] http://pomodorotechnique.com/

[24] de Manzano, Ö., Theorell, T., Harmat, L., Ullén, F. (2010). "The
psychophysiology of flow during piano playing." *Emotion* 10 (3): 301–311. DOI:
10.1037/a0018432.

[25] Vozza, S. (2014, May 27). How To Hack Into Your Flow State And Quintuple
Your Productivity. Retrieved March 14, 2016, from
http://www.fastcompany.com/3031052/the-future-of-work/how-to-hack-into-your-
flow-state-and-quintuple-your-productivity

[26] Multitasking ability can be improved through training. (2009, July 15). Retrieved March 14, 2016, from http://news.vanderbilt.edu/2009/07/multitasking-ability-can-be-improved-through-training-84357/

[27] Weinschenk, S. (2012, September 18). The True Cost Of Multi-Tasking. Retrieved March 14, 2016, from https://www.psychologytoday.com/blog/brain-wise/201209/the-true-cost-multi-tasking

[28] C. J., Boyce, G. D.A., Brown, S. C., Moore (2010). "Money and Happiness: Rank of Income, Not Income, Affects Life Satisfaction." *Psychological Science* 21 (4): 471–475. DOI: 10.1177/0956797610362671

[29] Solnick, S. J., Hemenway D. (1998). "Is more always better?: A survey on positional concerns." *Journal of Economic Behavior & Organization* 37: 373–383. DOI: 10.1016/S0167-2681(98)00089-4.

[30] El Issa, E. American Household Credit Card Debt Statistics: 2015 - NerdWallet. Retrieved March 15, 2016, from https://www.nerdwallet.com/blog/credit-card-data/average-credit-card-debt-household/

[31] Doing Good Is Good for You. 2013 Health and Volunteering Study. Retrieved March 16, 2016, from http://www.unitedhealthgroup.com/~/media/UHG/PDF/2013/UNH-Health-Volunteering-Study.ashx

[32] What is the value of a vacation? | Tony Robbins. Retrieved March 16, 2016, from https://www.youtube.com/watch?v=bzrTITvD_X4

[33] 62% of Americans Have Less Than $1,000 in Savings, Survey Finds | GOBankingRates. (2015, October 05). Retrieved March 16, 2016, from http://www.gobankingrates.com/savings-account/62-percent-americans-under-1000-savings-survey-finds/

[34] Schwartz, T. (2013, February 09). Relax! You'll Be More Productive. Retrieved March 17, 2016, from http://www.nytimes.com/2013/02/10/opinion/sunday/relax-youll-be-more-productive.html?pagewanted=all

[35] Insufficient Sleep Is a Public Health Problem. (2015, September 03). Retrieved March 19, 2016, from http://www.cdc.gov/features/dssleep/index.html

[36] Schoenborn, C. A, Adams, P. F. (2010). "Health behaviors of adults: United States, 2005–2007." *Vital and Health Statistics* 10 (245).

[37] Van Dongen, H. P., Maislin, G., Mullington, J. M., Dinges, D. F. (2003). "The cumulative cost of additional wakefulness: dose-response effects on neurobehavioral functions and sleep physiology from chronic sleep restriction and total sleep deprivation." *Sleep* 26 (2): 117–126.

[38] Lauderdale, D. S., Knutson, K. L., Yan, L. L., Liu K., Rathouz, P. J. (2008). "Sleep duration: how well do self-reports reflect objective measures? The CARDIA Sleep Study." *Epidemiology* 19 (6): 838–845. DOI: 10.1097/EDE.0b013e318187a7b0.

[39] Expedia's 2015 Vacation Deprivation Study: Europe Leads World in Paid Vacation Time While Americans and Asians Lag | Expedia Viewfinder. (2015, November 16). Retrieved March 21, 2016, from https://viewfinder.expedia.com/news/expedia-s-2015-vacation-deprivation-study-europe-leads-world-in-paid-vacation-time-while-americans-and-asians-lag/

[40] Vacation's Impact on the Workplace. Retrieved March 21, 2016, from http://www.projecttimeoff.com/research/vacation's-impact-workplace

[41] Zenger, J., Folkman, J. (2015, June 17). Are We More Productive When We Have More Time Off? Retrieved March 21, 2016, from https://hbr.org/2015/06/are-we-more-productive-when-we-have-more-time-off

[42] The Work Martyr's Affair: How America's Lost Week Quietly Threatens Our Relationships. Retrieved March 21, 2016, from http://www.projecttimeoff.com/research/work-martyrs-affair-how-americas-lost-week-quietly-threatens-our-relationships

[43] The OEC: Facts about the language. Retrieved March 17, 2016, from http://www.oxforddictionaries.com/words/the-oec-facts-about-the-language

[44] American Time Use Survey – 2014 Results. (2015, June 24). Retrieved March 23, 2016, from http://www.bls.gov/news.release/pdf/atus.pdf

[45] Mattson M. P., Wan R. (2005). "Beneficial effects of intermittent fasting and caloric restriction on the cardiovascular and cerebrovascular systems." *The Journal of Nutritional Biochemistry* 16 (3): 129–137. DOI: 10.1016/j.jnutbio.2004.12.007.

[46] Martin B., Mattson M. P., Maudsley S. (2006). "Caloric restriction and intermittent fasting: Two potential diets for successful brain aging." *Ageing Research Reviews* 5 (3): 332–353. DOI: 10.1016/j.arr.2006.04.002.

[47] Heilbronn L. K, Smith S. R., Martin, Corby K., Anton S. D, Ravussin E. (2005). "Alternate-day fasting in nonobese subjects: Effects on body weight, body composition, and energy metabolism." *The American Journal of Clinical Nutrition* 81 (1): 69–73.

[48] Klempel M. C., Kroeger C. M., Varady K. A. (2013). "Alternate day fasting (ADF) with a high-fat diet produces similar weight loss and cardio-protection as ADF with a low-fat diet." *Metabolism* 62 (1): 137–43. DOI: 10.1016/j.metabol.2012.07.002.

[49] von Thiele Schwarz, U.; Hasson, H. (2011); "Employee self-rated productivity and objective organizational production levels: effects of worksite health interventions involving reduced work hours and physical exercise." *Journal of Occupational and Environmental Medicine* 53 (8): 838–44. DOI: 10.1097/JOM.0b013e31822589c2.

[50] Puetz, T. W.; Flowers, S. S.; O'Connor, P. J. (2008); "A randomized controlled trial of the effect of aerobic exercise training on feelings of energy and fatigue in

sedentary young adults with persistent fatigue." *Psychotherapy and Psychosomatics* 77 (3): 167–74. DOI: 10.1159/000116610.

[51] Craft, L. L; Perna, F. M. (2004); "The benefits of exercise for the clinically depressed." *Primary Care Companion to the Journal of Clinical Psychiatry* 6 (3): 104–111.

[52] Broman-Fulks, J. J.; Berman, M. E.; Rabian, B. A.; Webster M. J. (2004); "Effects of aerobic exercise on anxiety sensitivity." *Behaviour Research and Therapy* 42 (2): 125–136. DOI: 10.1016/S0005-7967(03)00103-7.

[53] Carek, P. J.; Laibstain, S. E.; Carek, S. M. (2011); "Exercise for the treatment of depression and anxiety." *International Journal of Psychiatry in Medicine* 41 (1): 15–28. DOI: 10.2190/PM.41.1.c.

[54] Elavsky, S. (2010); "Longitudinal examination of the exercise and self-esteem model in middle-aged women." *Journal of Sport & Exercise Psychology* 32 (6): 862–80.

[55] Pretty, J., Peacock, J., Sellens, M., Griffin, M. (2005); "The mental and physical health outcomes of green exercise." *International Journal of Environmental Health Research* 15 (5): 319–37. DOI: 10.1080/09603120500155963.

[56] Griffin, É. W.; Mullally, S.; Foley, C.; Warmington, S. A.; O'Mara S. M.; Kelly A. M. (2011); "Aerobic exercise improves hippocampal function and increases BDNF in the serum of young adult males." *Physiology and Behavior* 104 (5): 934–41. DOI: 10.1016/j.physbeh.2011.06.005.

[57] Intlekofer, K. A.; Cotman, C. W. (2013); "Exercise counteracts declining hippocampal function in aging and Alzheimer's disease." *Neurobiology of disease* 57: 47–55. DOI: 10.1016/j.nbd.2012.06.011.

[58] Steinberg, H.; Sykes, E. A.; Moss, T.; Lowery, S.; LeBoutillier, N.; Dewey, A. (1997); "Exercise enhances creativity independently of mood." *British Journal of Sports Medicine* 31: 240–245. DOI: 10.1136/bjsm.31.3.240.

[59] Youngstedt, S. D. (2005); "Effects of exercise on sleep." *Clinics in sports medicine* 24 (2): 355–65. DOI: 10.1016/j.csm.2004.12.003.

Lightning Source UK Ltd.
Milton Keynes UK
UKHW010256090223
416650UK00002B/341

9 788395 298707